An illustrated souvenir
SUTTON HOUSE
Hackney

Mike Gray

National Trust

Introduction

Built for a Tudor courtier about 1535, Sutton House has, at various times, been the home of wool and silk merchants, girls' and boys' boarding schools, a home for several Huguenot families, a house for the Hackney Vestry Chief Clerk, a Church Institute, a trades union headquarters and a squat for the homeless. Its history reflects the changing condition of Hackney, from a village in the 16th century, providing a healthy country retreat for London's rich, to a cosmopolitan inner London borough in the late 20th century.

Sutton House takes its name from Sir Thomas Sutton, who founded Charterhouse School in 1611 and was once thought to have owned the house, but it has been called many things over nearly 500 years: 'the bryk place', Milford, Ivy and Picton Houses, 'the Old House at the Corner', St John's Institute and 'the Blue House'. It has the distinction of being the oldest domestic building in the East End of London.

Sutton House has survived because it has been able to adapt to its changing social environment. It has now recovered from a period of dereliction and decay in the 1980s to become a cultural and social centre for the 21st century after a restoration and rehabilitation programme costing over £2m.

The Young National Trust Theatre performing at Sutton House

Sutton House in 1994 after restoration

Tudor Hackney

The ragstone tower of St Augustine's, all that now remains of the former parish church

On 3 October 1537 Ralph Sadleir, one of Henry VIII's Privy Councillors, wrote to Thomas Cromwell, his master and patron, explaining his absence from Hampton Court. Fearing that Sadleir might have contracted the plague from a sick servant, the King had sent him home to Hackney. Sadleir informed Cromwell that 'the plague reiynese in dyvers partes of London and in dyvers villages about London But thankes be god – Hackeney was never clerer than it is at this present.'

Less than three miles across open fields from Bishopsgate in the City, Hackney was noted for its 'healthful air', no doubt a reason why many courtiers and wealthy London merchants chose the village for their country retreats. Sadleir's Hackney home was a newly built red-brick mansion called, appropriately, 'the bryk place'. It stood within an estate of about 30-acres in the hamlet of Homberton (Homerton), just to the east of the parish church of St Augustine's. The ragstone tower of this church, founded by the Knights Templar in the 13th century, still stands.

In Clapton, about half a mile to the north of the church, was a very substantial double courtyard house known as 'the King's Place'. (Later called Brooke House, it was demolished in 1954.) Dating at least from the 1470s, it was largely rebuilt by Thomas Cromwell in 1535. A year later it was the setting for a historic meeting between Henry VIII and his estranged daughter Mary. She was persuaded at that time to sign articles declaring that she had been born illegitimate. 'Mary was braught rydinge from Hunsedonne secretelye in the nyght to Hacknaye'. She 'had not spoken with the Kinge her father in five yere afore,' wrote Charles Wriothesley. In 1547 Sadleir himself came into possession of the King's Place as he progressively extended his landholdings in the parish.

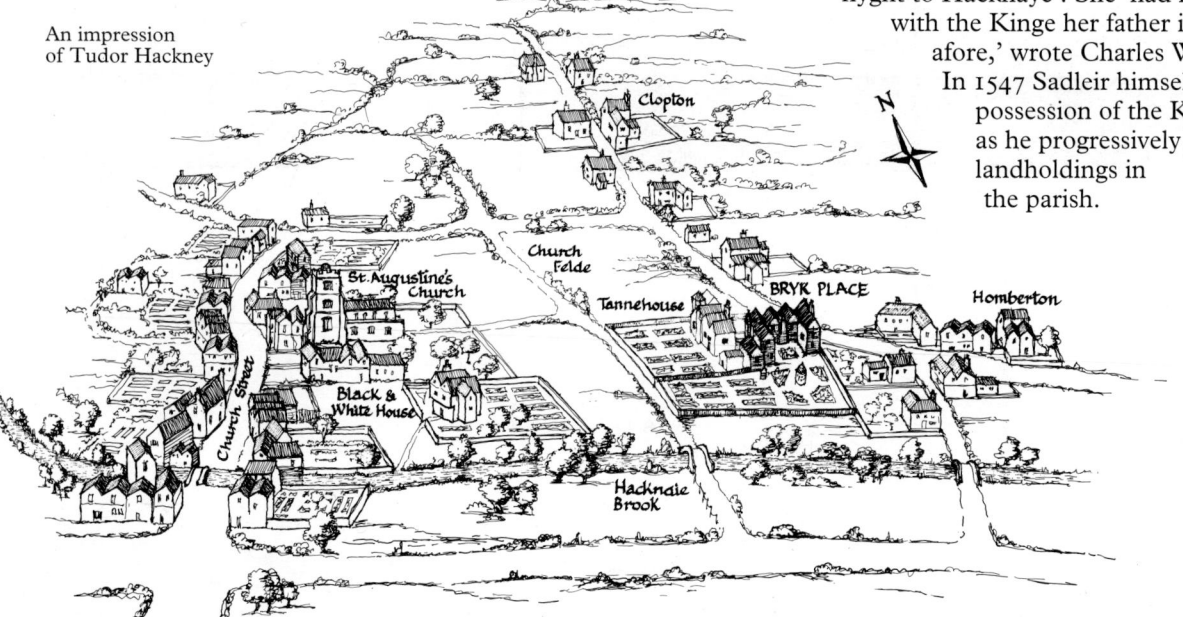

An impression of Tudor Hackney

Detail from an 18th-century engraving of 'the King's Place', later known as Brooke House

Sir Ralph Sadleir – Soldier, Diplomat

Portrait of an unknown man, thought to be Ralph Sadleir, by Holbein, 1535 (Royal Collection)

Sir Ralph Sadleir was born in 1507, according to the inscription on his magnificent tomb in the parish church of Standon, near Ware in Hertfordshire, which continues:

> Here lieth ingraved Sr Rafe Sadleir Knighte by God and ye Kinge calde to that degree, a meane gentilman of name by his birthe righte yet in his time so rewarded was he for service done wch was due to doe first to God nexte to his prince and contree whiche oughte to move all such as ar borne so...

Ralph's family came from Warwickshire where his father Henry was steward to Sir Edward Belknapp, an important Warwickshire landowner. In 1520 Belknapp was charged with planning arrangements for the Field of Cloth of Gold, the spectacular tournament held near Calais to celebrate the meeting of King Henry and Francis I of France. Henry Sadleir was appointed purveyor of all the buckram and canvas that this extravagant temporary construction of pavilions and palaces required. Within a year Sadleir had bought a house in Hackney, probably on the site of the present Sutton House. This building had previously been a brewery or tavern.

In order to secure the lease Henry Sadleir needed to redeem a debt and called upon his good friend Thomas Cromwell to help him. He wrote:

> ...Syr, I shoyd your mastreship howe I have boughte a howse in Haceney. And I thanke almyghtty God I have payde for it with yn 8L 2s [£8 2s]. That payde I trust I my wyfe and our childryn shall inioye the saied howse with the appurtenences to godly plesure...

Detail of Ralph Sadleir's tomb in Standon church, Hertfordshire, showing his seven children but not his wife

Thomas Cromwell, after Holbein (National Portrait Gallery)

At this time Ralph was fourteen and had been placed in the household of Thomas Cromwell at his city home in Fenchurch Street. Here he learnt Latin and developed the other skills he would later put to use in his political career. Sadleir rapidly became Cromwell's right-hand man and prospered with his master. He was first mentioned in State Papers in 1527 as secretary to Cromwell, but by 1535 he was directly in the King's service, having carried out many missions in connection with the Dissolution of the Monasteries. He was later sent on embassies to Scotland and France.

At Cromwell's house Sadleir met Helen Barre, a cousin of Thomas Cromwell but in reduced circumstances because her husband had deserted her and their two children. It was believed that he had died later in Ireland. Ralph and Helen married in 1533, and by 1535 Ralph had built his family a three-storey house in Hackney, 'the bryk place'. In that year he wrote to Cromwell asking him to be godfather to his son Thomas, who was to be baptised in Hackney church:

> My wife, after long travaile, and as payneful labour as any woman could have, hathe at the laste brought furth a fayre boy; beseeching you to vouchsafe ones agayne to be gossip [godfather] unto so poore a man as I am.

The Field of Cloth of Gold; by an unknown 16th-century artist (Royal Collection)

The effigy of Sir Ralph Sadleir in Standon church

An account book written in Latin describes Ralph Sadleir's estate in 1540. It consisted of a mansion on the south side of 'Hamerton Streete' 'built with beautiful buildings' (presumably 'bryk place'); a house to the west side of the mansion, then occupied by his father Henry, which had been a tannery (tanhouse); a small house at the back of the latter and another house on the north of the street. Sometime after 1540 Sadleir acquired or built another house 50 metres to the east of 'bryk place', similar to it in plan, but probably one storey lower.

In 1540 Sadleir was knighted and became Principal Secretary of State to Henry. However, his career faltered briefly when, on Cromwell's arrest for treason that year, Sadleir was also arrested and sent to the Tower 'with hands tightly bound, and under a guard of 24 armed men'. He was released soon afterwards and, dissociating himself from Cromwell, resumed his court duties apparently unscathed.

By 1544 he and his wife had seven surviving children, but their future was jeopardised by two dramatic events. Sadleir was that year sent as ambassador to Scotland, although he had little regard for the Scots. He wrote from Edinburgh, 'Under the sun live not more beastly and unreasonable people than be here', an attitude perhaps influenced by the musket ball which narrowly missed him while he was walking in his garden there.

Meanwhile, a man appeared in London claiming to be Helen's first husband. An enquiry was called and the claim upheld. Sadleir returned in haste from Scotland and managed to obtain an Act of Parliament annulling Helen's first marriage, so averting the shame of seven illegitimate children.

reigns of Edward VI and Elizabeth, although as a Protestant he lived in retirement between 1553 and 1558 under the Catholic Queen Mary. One of his final tasks was as a judge at the trial of Mary, Queen of Scots in 1586. He died the next year at the age of 80. His career was summed up by the 17th-century historian David Lloyd:

> [He] saw the interest of the state altered six times, and died an honest man; the crown was put upon four heads, yet he continued a faithful subject; religion changed five times, yet he kept his faith. He was a most exquisite writer, and a most valiant soldier, a qualification that is seldom met, so great is the distance between the sword and the pen.

(*Far left*) Henry VIII, circle of Holbein (Petworth House, Sussex)

(*Left*) The trial of Mary, Queen of Scots, 1586. Sadleir, one of Mary's judges, is no. 29 in this early drawing (British Library)

By 1546 Sadleir had built a new and grander mansion at Standon near Ware in Hertfordshire, and in 1550 he sold his Hackney property, including 'bryk place', to a wealthy wool merchant, John Machell.

Sadleir's diplomatic career continued after Henry's death in 1547 through the

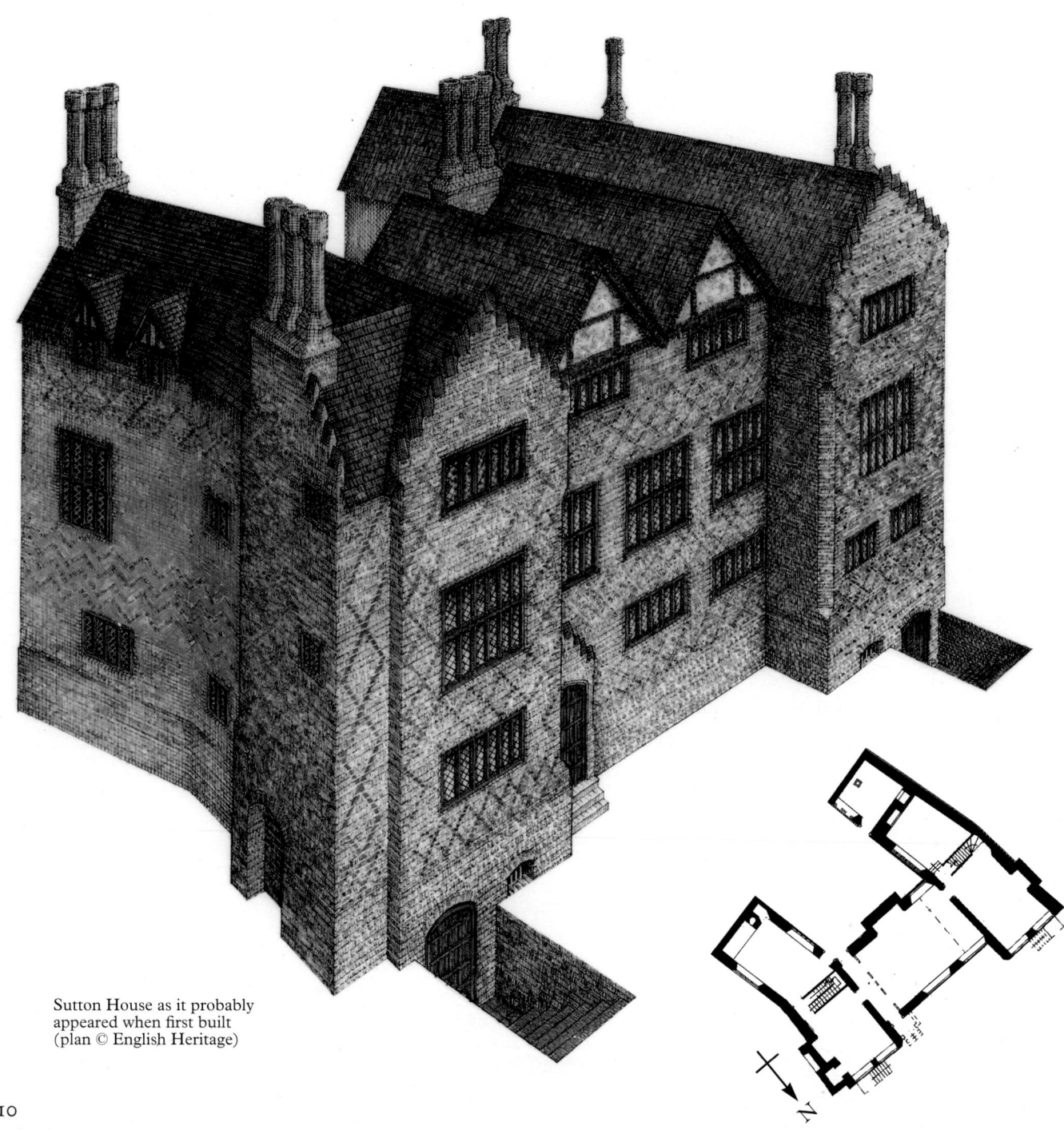

Sutton House as it probably appeared when first built (plan © English Heritage)

The house that Ralph built

Recent tree-ring analysis of the timbers in Sutton House enables us with some confidence to ascribe to it a building date of 1534–5. This fits in well with the fact that Sadleir's mentor, Thomas Cromwell, was rebuilding nearby King's Place at that time. One hundred oaks from the royal forest at Enfield had been given to Cromwell by the King and it seems likely that some may have been used at Ralph's Homerton site. Houses built in south-east England during the early 16th century were mostly timber-framed with infilling of wattle and daub. Sutton House's original name – 'bryk place' – indicates how unusual such brick houses were in Hackney at that time.

Sadleir built his house in the familiar Tudor 'H' plan, with two wings separated by a central range. However, because of older buildings retained close to the site, the rear of both wings had to be built askew. The brickwork was decorated up to the second-floor level with 'diapering' – over-fired black bricks arranged, as was the fashion, to create lozenge and diamond patterns. The bricks were around two inches in depth – typical of the period but narrower by about half an inch than most later bricks. The bricks were made from brickearth, a fine clay, dug from the banks of Hackney Brook nearby.

The windows were constructed in oak with vertical bars or mullions. The largest windows on the first floor would also have had one horizontal bar (a transom), like the window which survives in the central courtyard. The windows at ground-floor level at the front of the house were all very high off the ground, well above head height, providing security and privacy at a time when the streets were roamed by 'rogues and vagabonds'.

At the roof line were four gables, the middle two half-timbered and decorated with carved wooden bargeboards. They and the window frames were painted maroon to blend with the brickwork. The service end, with kitchen and buttery, was on the east of the house. A Great Hall, which filled the central range at ground-floor level, linked the service wing to the parlour, with its linenfold panelled walls, on the west. In the London area, only Hampton Court Palace and Westminster Abbey have similar panelled rooms dating from the early 16th century. Many of the rooms had carved stone fireplaces, four of which survive. The kitchen fireplace was open under a wide oak lintel, most of which has also survived.

The Great Hall, where most meals would have been taken, had a dais at the west end for the high table, and the floor was paved with foot-square red tiles. An oak front door opened into a screens passage on the east side of the Hall. This door was moved to its present position on the west side in the 18th century.

The finely panelled Great Chamber was above the Great Hall. It was reached by a steep, narrow stairway in the west wing, and led, at the east end, to the principal bedchamber, with its own privy. On the top floor under the roof were rooms for the household servants and children. The two cellars under the wings were accessible from the outside. The brick niches are thought to have been used for storing casks of ale or wine. The brick well which supplied the house with water still survives. It is beside the new conservatory.

The Tudor window in the west wing, in a drawing of 1904

The brick relieving arch of the original Tudor fireplace was revealed when the linenfold panelling was taken down

The Sheriff of London's house

John Machell was born around 1509 in Kendal, Westmorland. As a young man he came to London and served an apprenticeship in the cloth trade. In 1530 he was admitted to the Freedom of the Clothworkers' Company, one of the twelve principal livery companies, and had risen to the rank of Master by 1548.

About that time he purchased 421 bales of 'fustyans', or coarse cotton, from the Crown. The King's agent in such deals was probably Sir Ralph Sadleir, who by then was Master of the Great Wardrobe. In 1550 Machell purchased, for £500, most of Sadleir's Hackney estate including 'bryk place' and the old tanhouse. A deed describing the deal, now in the Guildhall Library, refers to:

> Alle that Capital messuage with th' appertanence of old tyme called a Breuhouse and afterwards a dwelling house in Hakeney aforesaid and now called the bryk place with almaner of lands, ten'ts, medowes, pastures, and feedings to the same belonging or appertaining or with the same now being occupied.

According to another document, the estate also had barns, stables, a dovecote and gardens bounded by Hackney Brook on the south.

In 1555 Machell was appointed Sheriff of London and was Lord Mayor designate in 1558, when, on 12 August, he died at his town house in Milk Street. He was buried with great pomp in the church of St Mary Magdalene nearby. His wife Jane inherited the house in Hackney, as their sons John, Mathew and Thomas were still minors.

On Jane's death in 1565, John Machell the younger came into possession of 'bryk place', and Mathew the tanhouse, which was first let, and eventually sold, to Francis Bowyer, a rich London merchant. There were frequent disputes between the brothers and Bowyer over this property. On 6 July 1577 John wrote to Bowyer:

> I have talked with my brother Mathew Machell, meating with him at the Church this afternoone, who stormed rather lyk a myd sumer morn, th' of sobrietie. He so fell out with me concerning your house as it was straunge. He meaneth as he sayeth to enter your house with force and therefore I think it good that you caused some body to lye the night [there].

A memorial in the old church records a family tragedy three years earlier:

> In this church was buried Frances, the wife of John Machell of Hackney esq. – dyed at her house in Hamerton May 11th 1574, in childbed. Deliver'd of two children, John son & heir and Frances. Buried May 21st.

Machell later married Ursula, daughter of Sir Francis Hynde, a rich Cambridgeshire landowner. The last document linking Machell with 'bryk place' is a note of 1605 granting Thomas Sutton land on which to build a brick wall between their properties.

In the Little Chamber

The coats of arms of the Machell family and the Clothworkers' Company, superimposed on John Machell's purchase Deed, which describes 'ye bryk place'

Go to Jail!

John Machell jnr. was at the height of his power and influence in the 1590s: he was a Justice of the Peace for Middlesex and played a major part in parish affairs in Hackney where he was one of the highest rated residents. However, he seems to have over-reached himself when, in 1591, he purchased a large estate in Cambridgeshire. To do so he was obliged to mortgage 'bryk place' and 18 acres of land to Edward Holmeden, a member of the Grocers' Company and a Hackney resident. Machell later borrowed more money to pay off Holmeden, this time from Sir James Deane, a money-lender. Deane was a Master of the Drapers' Company and a founder of the East India Company and appears by the end of the 1590s to have been living in the house a little to the east of 'bryk place'. The debt was never repaid and in 1598 Deane took possession of 'bryk place', but claimed that a party of Machell's followers led by his wife Ursula and armed with swords and halberds came and seized the house back. Machell was pursued by Deane through the courts but somehow managed to hold on to 'bryk place' until 1606, when he finally lost possession of the house when he was arrested for debt and thrown into the King's Bench prison in Southwark. He remained there for six years during which time Ursula, his wife, appears to have stayed on in the house under the protection of her brother, William Hynde, a Member of Parliament, presumably with the consent of her neighbour Sir James Deane.

John Machell died in Cambridgeshire in 1624, 'worn out with care and grief for his great losses'. In spite of many attempts, the family never managed to regain its Hackney properties. Deane had died in 1608 and was buried in St Olave's Hart Street in London. He bequeathed 'bryk place' to his niece, Olive Clark, who married, rather confusingly, another James Deane. They lived in Hampshire and were almost certainly absentee landlords.

Sir James Deane's memorial in St Olave's Hart Street. He is shown with his third wife, Elizabeth. Their two children died in infancy, as indicated by the swaddling clothes in which they are wrapped.

Why 'Sutton House'?

Until recently it was widely believed that Thomas Sutton lived in the house now known as Sutton House. However, deeds and unpublished plans in the Charterhouse archives show that he lived next door, in the old tanhouse, which was eventually demolished in 1805 to make way for the fine Georgian terrace known as Sutton Place.

Thomas Sutton had moved to Hackney from the neighbouring parish of Stoke Newington in 1605, after the death of his wife. Through investments in coal mines in Durham and other extensive landholdings, Sutton had become one of the wealthiest commoners in the country. During the closing years of his life he refurbished the old Carthusian monastery in Clerkenwell, founding Charterhouse Hospital and School there in 1611. When he died at his Hackneyhouse in December that year, his entrails were buried in the old churchyard. It was three years before his embalmed body was finally put to rest in the chapel at Charterhouse beneath a splendid monument. Sutton bequeathed his Hackney house and its one-acre garden to the Governors of Charterhouse who retained the property until the 1930s.

Thomas Sutton. The diarist John Aubrey later wrote: 'Twas from him that [Ben] Jonson took his hint of the fox and by Signor Volpone is meant Sutton.' Sutton himself is recorded as praying: 'Lord thou hast given me a large and liberal estate. Give me also the heart to make use of thereof.'

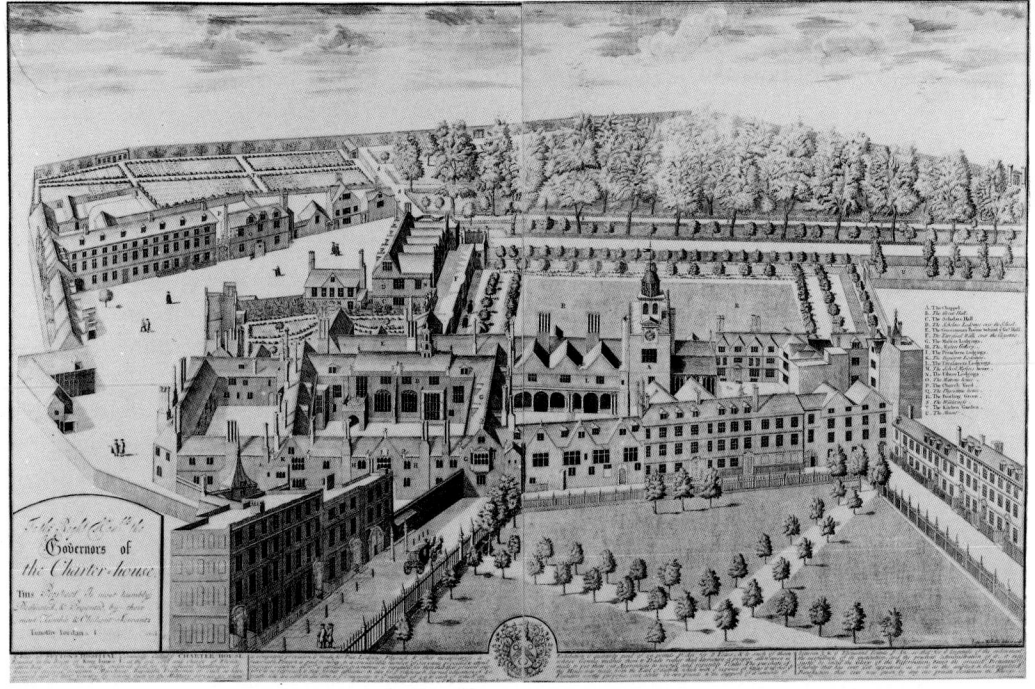

The Charterhouse; engraving by Sutton Nicholl, c.1750

The Rise and Fall of Captain Milward

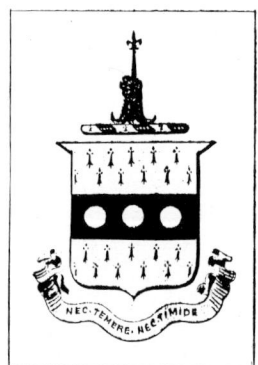

Armorial bearings of the Milward family which appear on one of the Tudor fireplaces and in several other places at Sutton House

Detail of the strapwork wall painting on the west staircase, c.1630

During archaeological work at the house in 1988 a Tudor stone fireplace was discovered on the first floor of the west wing. It had been bricked in and a staircase fitted in front of it in the 18th century. Underneath layers of limewash was a well-preserved 17th-century gilded and painted decoration applied to the stonework, incorporating the coats of arms of the Milward and Shrigley families. Milwards were certainly living in Hackney at this time, for Vestry minutes record that on 17 August 1634 a Captain John Milward applied for a pew in Hackney Church 'to himselfe during his aboade in this Parish'. Clearly Milward now owned the house, but nothing is yet known about the connection of the Shrigley family with the house and with the Milwards.

The house had possibly become known as Milward House. This name, however, does not occur in any known documents but is inferred from the fact that a later name, Milford House, appears to be a corruption of Milward.

A token found at Sutton House, issued by John Pepiatt, landlord of the Mermaid, a local inn, c.1640

Captain Milward was a silk merchant with wide interests in the City. He also commanded a company of the London Trained Bands, forerunners of the City of London militia. Milward extensively redecorated the house in the brightest of colours. Elaborate strapwork wall-paintings lined a new west stairway incorporating cherubs, griffins and his coat of arms. The linenfold panelling was painted corn yellow against a field of emerald green, and the frames mahogany red with stencilled gold floral motifs. The house was furnished with silk carpets brought from the Far East.

Milward also owned the house nearby, formerly the home of Sir James Deane. Here until her death in 1634 lived Frances Rich, the Dowager Countess of Warwick. Milward's daughter, Elizabeth, married Edward, the son of Sir Maurice Abbott, Governor of the East India Company and brother of the Archbishop of Canterbury. The Milwards were clearly moving in the most exalted circles but this did not save Captain John when a collapse in silk prices led to failure of his business. In 1639 he made over his estate to his son-in-law and died soon after. Thomas Milward, John's son, continued to live in the house with his second wife Jane until Edward Abbott, in his turn, was declared bankrupt in 1642. He fled with Elizabeth to Pisa. Thomas Milward with his family and his mother Ann lived on in one or both of the houses by arrangement with the assignees in bankruptcy. By 1655 Thomas had died and the next year the estate, including Milward House, was surrendered to the Lord of the Manor of Hackney who then granted the copyhold to a Henry Whittingham of St Helen's Bishopsgate.

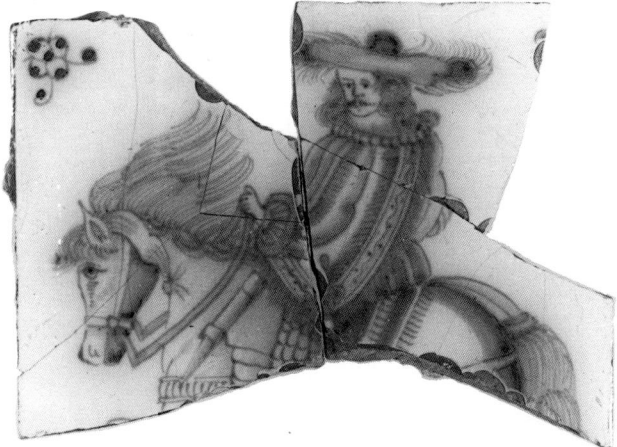

Fragment of a late 17th-century Delft tile found in the cellar

Ships trading in the east, detail from a painting by Hendrick Vroom, (National Maritime Museum)

Schooldays

Samuel Pepys; painted by John Hayls, 1666 (National Portrait Gallery)

Hackney church in the 18th century

Henry Whittingham was born in Islington and prospered sufficiently well to own a large house in Bishopsgate which, during the Civil War, had been commandeered by Cromwell's soldiers for he was known to be a royalist sympathiser. Whittingham had offered his nephew to Charles I with the recommendation that he 'is tall enough to do you service, he hath a Spanish blade by his side, and a Welsh heart in his body; I wish they should agree to conquer your enemies'.

Whittingham appears to have bought 'Milward House' as an investment rather than as an alternative dwelling for himself because by November 1657 he had leased the house to Sarah Freeman, a widow, who established a girls' school there. She must have been fairly well provided for to pay the high rent and also the cost of a gallery in the parish church for her scholars. In 1672 the Parish Vestry ordered that 'Mrs Freeman shall have the libertie to build a gallery and to remaine to her and one Daughter [Priscilla] soo long as they keepe schoole in Hackney'. In 1674 Sarah paid 48s hearth tax, that is to say 2 shillings for each of 24 hearths. A tax on fireplaces was levied between 1662 and 1689. Tax returns for that year show that only three or four houses in the parish had more hearths. The unpopularity of this tax in Hackney can be judged by the case of William Burrett who was sent to the Fleet Prison 'for assaulting the Headborough of Hackney and the Officers collecting the hearth money, and for inciting the people against payment of that duty'.

Sarah Freeman's girls' school was one of several in the village of Hackney in the latter part of the 17th century. Indeed, Hackney became known as 'The Ladies' University of Female Arts'. So many schoolgirls packed into Hackney church on Sundays that the Vestry received a complaint that there were not enough seats for ordinary parishioners. Samuel Pepys was pleased by the spectacle and did not seem to mind the crush. In 1667 he 'then took coach and to Hackney church, where very full. . . . That which we went chiefly to see was the young ladies of the schools, whereof there is great store, very pretty'. John Aubrey, on the other hand, condemned the Hackney schools as places 'where young maids learnt pride and wantonness'. Mrs Freeman's school lasted at least until 1694 when it was included in a list of well-known ladies' boarding schools in the London area.

The school itself continued into the 18th century when for some years it was kept by a Mrs Amy Hutton. Dudley Ryder, who later became Attorney General, was then a

HACKNEY CHURCH.

An 18th-century girls' school very similar to the one at 'Milward House'

young law student living in a house on the other side of Homerton Road. He recorded in his diary:

> August 23 1716 As I came home went to the back door of the schoolhouse in the field and there found Mr Hudson, Milbourn and Gould at the door. The girls were first very merry at dancing but presently comes the schoolmistress [Mrs Hutton] and reproved them very severely for their having held discourse with a man and entertaining them upon the wall.

By 1723 the school was taken over by a Mrs Mary Joseph who continued to run it until the year of her death in 1741 when, in her will, she left to her companion Sarah Baldwin, a set of cherry-coloured bed curtains lined with green which perhaps had hung in the house.

The Shock of the New

Shortly after Mary Joseph died, John Cox came into possession of the house and between 1741 and 1743 he made extensive alterations. Cox, who had been building new houses in Homerton for some years, bought 'Milward House' to modernise and let for a higher rent than he could obtain by leaving the house in its old-fashioned state.

The solid, heavy-looking mullioned windows were replaced by elegant sashes. The gables at the front of the house were hipped back and partially concealed behind a parapet and the large brick chimneys gave way to earthenware chimneypots. In the front room on the ground floor of the east wing, formerly the buttery,

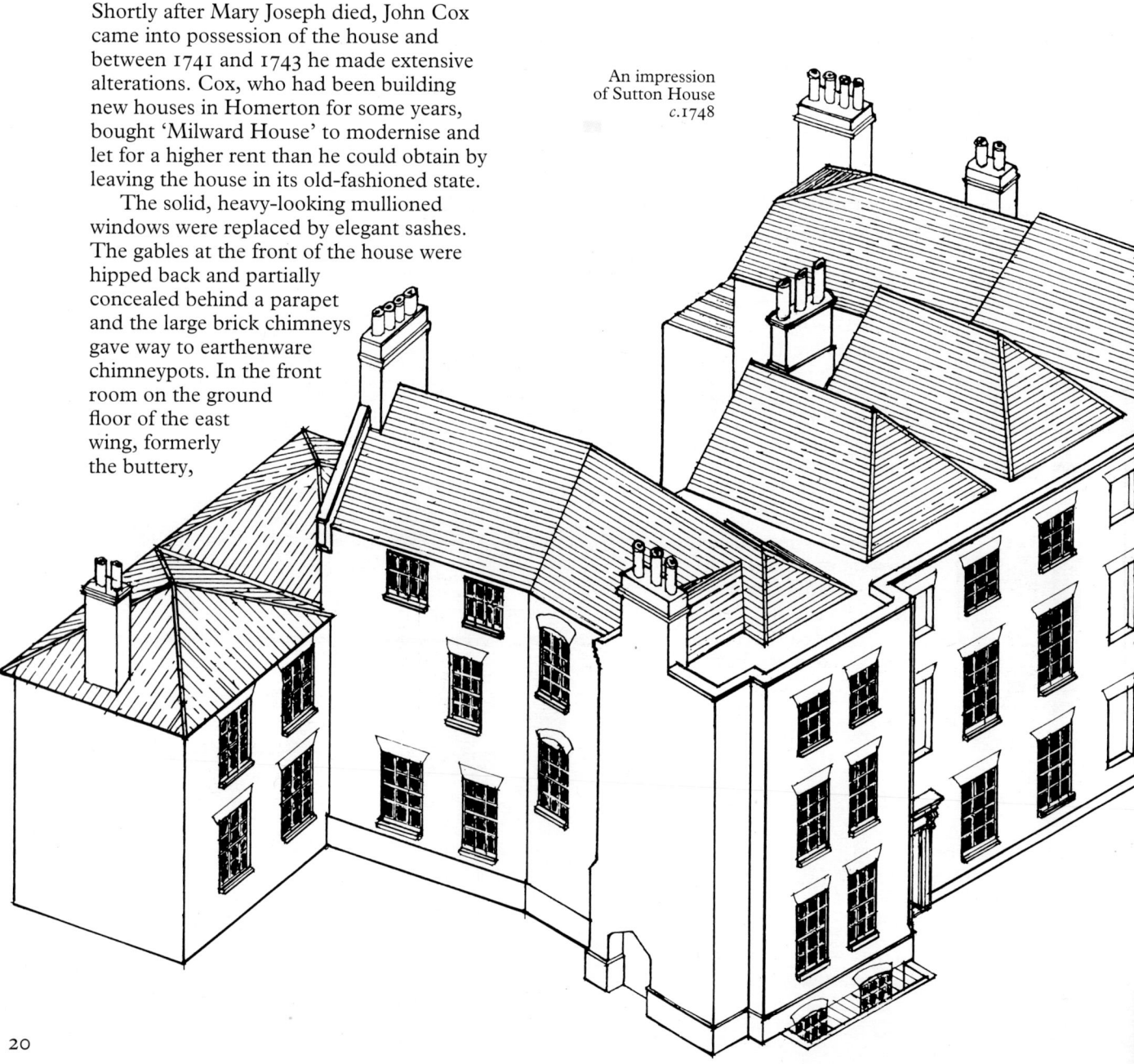

An impression of Sutton House *c.*1748

a cloth wall-covering was replaced by large Baltic pine panels and a fine box-cornice inserted. All the stone fireplaces were replaced by new surrounds with iron grates, usually leaving the old ones in place behind. At the end of the work very few of the Tudor features remained visible. Fortunately the work was carried out in an economical way and many of these features were simply covered or painted over, to be revealed again by later owners.

In 1743, with the work completed, a new tenant's name appeared in the rate book, Mrs Mary Tooke (née Lethieullier), a wealthy widow whose husband, Edmund Tooke, had been Clerk of the Salters' Company. She belonged to a family of very prominent Huguenot merchants. She was the first of many occupants of the house who were of French Protestant descent, having fled from persecution in Catholic France.

By 1748 it seems that Cox had also built a two-storey cottage attached to the rear of the east wing of 'Milward House'. The tenant was a Mr Timothy Ravenhill whose name was probably derived from the French name Ravenell.

A 1904 photograph of the library in the east wing. The panelling, cornice and fireplace date from the mid 18th century

The north front in the 1890s, showing the sash-windows inserted c.1743

21

'The Upper Clapton Macaroni', a fashionable Hackney gentleman of the 1790s

A House Divided

Mary Tooke died in 1751 leaving £10,000 to her grown-up children, a considerable fortune in those days. Cox then divided the mansion into two self-contained residences and enlarged the east wing by knocking through into the new cottage. Ravenhill took over the eastern house which was known as Ivy House and Colonel George Garrett, from a family of Spitalfields silkweavers, briefly lived in the house on the west side. This house, which at some time became known as Milford House, occupied most of the central range and the west wing, as well as a two-storey addition on the west. Corridors were inserted at both ends of the Great Hall, creating a new central room which was lined with large pine panels from floor to ceiling. In the east wing a fine balustered staircase was put in. Probably at this time an entrance to the east house was opened from the east into what had been the Tudor kitchen. This room became a hall with a plaster cornice and an iron grate under the original great lintel of the open fireplace. The left-hand end of the lintel was sawn through and a stairway rising to the first floor of the cottage to the south was inserted.

The Hackney parish rate books provide a complete record of the occupants of the two houses from the 1750s. They all leased or rented the premises from a copyholder who owned several houses in the area. By 1758 Cox himself took up residence in Milford House and was succeeded by his daughter Sarah after his death in 1760.

In the 1760s Ivy House was occupied by another Huguenot family, that of John Newman Cousemaker. He and his wife brought up an orphan girl, Sarah Gay.

The ground-floor plan of Sutton House *c.*1750–1890 (© English Heritage)

▨ IVY HOUSE

▨ MILFORD HOUSE

Sarah's parents and the Cox family had been on close terms and by 1780 Sarah possessed the leases of Ivy House and some other houses nearby. In 1783 she married a young man, Nicholas de Ste Croix, who came originally from Jersey, where many French Protestants had settled. By 1790, after the Fruchards and Perigals (two families of French silk merchants) had been successive tenants, Sarah and her husband moved back into her old home, Ivy House, where they lived with their family until Nicholas's death in 1816. Their eldest son, William, first met his future wife, Mary Green, when she was visiting his sisters at Ivy House. Mary and the sisters were dancing in the hall as William arrived and they 'would not let him go and dress, but stop and dance then and there and he danced in his top boots!'

Nicholas de Ste Croix held a senior position at the Excise Office, although his occupation is not mentioned in his obituary in *The Gentleman's Magazine*. He seems to have left his family in impoverished circumstances as they were obliged to leave Ivy House soon after.

A young lady's glove, purse and shoe found under the floorboards

The 19th Century

In 1816 the east house was renamed Picton House in honour of General Picton a hero in the Napoleonic wars who had recently died at the Battle of Waterloo. By the early 1820s, and for over forty subsequent years, the occupant was Charles Horton Pulley, a solicitor. Pulley (from the French Poley) was Hackney's Vestry Clerk and holder of several other lucrative parochial posts, a fact that received criticism from some quarters. He threatened to horsewhip a local publisher, Charles Green, who in his *Hackney Magazine* of July 1834 accused Pulley of being 'a pluralist and a bungler'.

For many years the west house, Milford House, was leased by the family of Thomas and Henrietta Davies. Davies was Chief Clerk in the Navy Office, a post held many years before by Samuel Pepys. However by 1818 Milford House was once again a school, this time for boys, where the Rev. Dr Thomas Burnet FRS ran a 'first class gentlemen's boarding school'.

Burnet was a Scotsman born in Musselburgh and educated at Edinburgh University. He had two brothers, James and John, who were successful landscape painters. Thomas became Rector of the church of St James Garlickhythe in London, a parish he served for many years.

Several old boys of Dr Burnet's school reached some prominence in their careers, the most notable being the Victorian novelist Lord Lytton (Edward Bulwer-Lytton), author of the once popular *Last Days of Pompeii*. His presence in the school was, however, brief and unhappy. He was to recall in his autobiography that on one occasion, shortly after his arrival at the school, he was playing chess with his friend Hardiman when he became increasingly

A view of Hackney in the 1850s, showing the bridge of the newly opened North London railway line

Edward Bulwer-Lytton

irritated by Mr Toms, the assistant master, who was sitting at his desk whistling. Edward blurted out imperiously, 'keep that confounded whistling to yourself'. Furious at this insubordination Toms called the Head who, failing to frighten the boy, boxed his ears and received the same in return. Edward was accordingly 'condemned to solitary confinement' for two days on bread and water. He was eventually rescued by his mother, who took him away in her carriage and arranged for the rest of his education to be by a private tutor.

Dr Burnet left Homerton after his appointment as Rector of St James. From the 1830s until the 1870s Mrs Elizabeth Temple ran a girls' school at the premises. The 1851 census return records 26 boarders in the school. Examples of their needlework and writing exercises, as well as shoes and much-darned socks, have been found under floorboards during the restoration, no doubt swept there by lazy monitors.

St John's Institute (1890–1930)

By the end of the 19th century the essentially middle-class character of Hackney had changed. Factories were proliferating along the Lee Navigation, filling backland sites and even taking over the larger houses. Homes considered suitable for the lower middle classes were still being built, but better transport meant that the more well-to-do moved further out. The houses they left gradually became multi-occupied

In 1895 Canon Evelyn Gardiner, the Rector of St John-at-Hackney, purchased the two houses and reunited them. Milford and Picton Houses then became St John's Church Institute, popularly known as the 'Tute', a recreational club for 'men of all classes'.

Benjamin Clark, a Hackney doctor and antiquarian, visited the building soon after it was acquired and noted that 'wood and stone alike, and panelling too, have all been covered with paint, after the late churchwarden fashion, and equally execrable'.

Sutton House as it is today

The walls of the ground-floor room were also 'as carefully covered either with whitewash or some painted medium, to destroy as much of ancient beauty as possible'.

At this time many of the house's picturesque outbuildings were destroyed to make way for a new building for the Free & Parochial School in Isabella Road. The buttery, the larder, a conservatory, the old garden with its dovecote and and statues, as well as many fine trees, disappeared.

In 1900 the recently founded London County Council condemned the building as unsafe. An appeal was launched and raised £3,000 towards its repair and refurbishment. Inspired by the new Rector, the Rev. Algernon Lawley, later to become Lord Wenlock, a very fine Institute emerged. The renovations were sympathetically carried out by builders Patman & Fotheringham. Paint, plaster, paper and modern brickwork were removed to reveal the beautifully carved oak panelling and two of the ancient stone fireplaces. New additions, in the then fashionable Arts and Crafts style, were built to designs by Lionel Crane, son of Walter Crane, the designer friend of William Morris.

The new Wenlock Barn was built behind the main house and seated upwards of two hundred. Institute members had at their disposal social, reading, writing, billiard and committee rooms, a library and a photographic darkroom. Football, cricket, cycling and athletic clubs all had their headquarters here. Light refreshments (but, of course, no alcohol) were supplied at moderate prices. The 25 rooms included bedrooms where young men, including younger members of the clergy, lodged. A caretaker lived in a new addition to the west wing.

Photograph of the interior of the Wenlock Barn taken in 1904

The rear of Sutton House; by F.C. Varley

A view through the Tudor doorway by Varley

St. John-at-Hackney
Magazine.

TURRIS FORTITUDINIS

VISIT
of
H.R.H. The Prince of Wales.

Illustrated
Souvenir Edition.

All profits on the sale will be given to the Mayor of Hackney's Fund for the Relief of Distress through unemployment.

Price 6d.

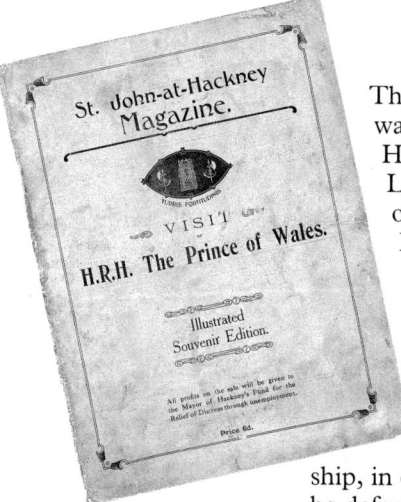

Souvenir issue of the St John-at-Hackney magazine for the visit of the Prince of Wales in 1926

The reopening of the Institute in 1904 was a grand affair. Lord Amherst of Hackney did the honours, with the Lord Mayor of London, the Mayor of Hackney and various old boys of Dr Burnet's school in attendance. Sir Arthur Lawley, brother of the Rector, planted a plane tree in the yard.

The parish magazine reported the event and Arthur Lawley's speech summrising the aims of the Institute as 'Friendship, in order that distrust in their minds be defeated by goodness, and all that concerned the healthy interests of young men, promoted. To this end, he hoped that some day the high ideals which they had set up for their Institute might be attained.' The Rev. C.B.H. Knight said that the Institute was intended for 'the development of the social and mental side, as well as the spiritual, of the men of Hackney'.

A new young curate, Francis Dent Vaisey, converted the east cellar into a chapel which was designed by Edward (later Sir Edward) Maufe, a church architect now best known for Guildford Cathedral. He also designed the altar and silver candlesticks. The chapel was dedicated by the Bishop of Stepney in 1914.

The visit of the Prince of Wales in April 1926 caused much local excitement. He insisted on shaking each member's hand as they filed past him in the Wenlock Barn. A full-length signed portrait of him hung thereafter in the Barn although it has long since disappeared.

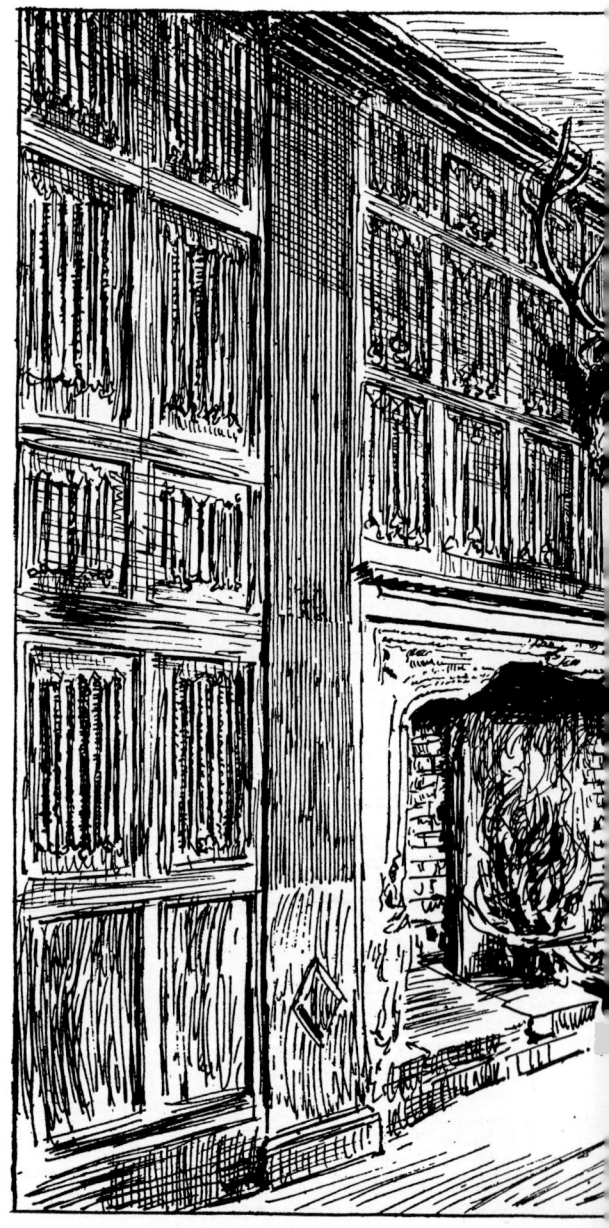

(*Right*) The linenfold panelling room as it was in 1936, drawn by Hanslip Fletcher

The president's room in 1904, now the Gallery

The inner courtyard c.1905, with the tree planted by Sir Arthur Lawley

Bought for the Nation

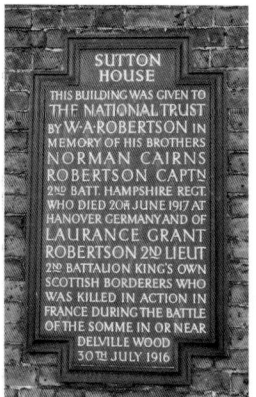

The memorial to the Robertson brothers on the front of the house

By 1936 the church had decided that the Institute needed new and more suitable club premises closer to the centre of Hackney. The house was initially offered to the Borough Council which carried out a survey, but decided against purchase.

An appeal was launched to save the house for the nation. The sponsors were Lord Crawford and Balcarres (President of both the London Society and the London Survey Committee), Lord Esher (Chairman of the Society for the Protection of Ancient Buildings) and George Lansbury (Vice-President of the National Trust and Labour MP for Poplar). The freehold was £2,500 and a further £500 was needed for urgent repairs. A tireless advocate of this campaign, and its principal fund-raiser, was Percy Lovell who was Secretary of both the London Survey Committee and the London Society. In these roles he played a very important part in the recording and safeguarding of London's historic buildings and, almost single-handedly, he ensured that the Institute would be protected.

Initially, however, the appeal fell short of its target and there was a real risk that the house would be sold privately and fall prey to developers. At the eleventh hour the National Trust was able to use the recently acquired Robertson bequest to purchase the house, and the funds raised by the appeal were spent on essential repairs and refurbishment. A plaque commemorating the Robertson brothers, who had died during the First World War and in whose memory the bequest had been made, is on the front of the house. Thus, in May 1938, ownership passed to the National Trust.

The house survived the London Blitz and throughout the Second World War was used as offices for a variety of charities and public services, including the Mission for the Relief of the Suffering Poor. This role continued into peacetime when it became the headquarters of Hackney Social Services. Its last tenant was the trade union ASTMS (the Association of Scientific, Technical and Managerial Staffs). It was during this period, in 1953, that the National Trust renamed St John's Institute 'Sutton House'.

When the union left the premises in 1982 the most vulnerable time in the house's history began. Despite repeated attempts, the National Trust was unable to find suitable tenants and the empty house was occupied by squatters, called 'the Blue House' and used for rock concerts. When the squatters were evicted, vandals and thieves moved in and removed fireplaces and the Tudor linenfold panelling which, fortunately, was later mostly recovered by a dealer and returned to the National Trust. As a precaution, the Trust took down the remaining panelling and put it into storage. Then the house was boarded up.

Graffiti, 1985

In some desperation, the National Trust entered into negotiations with a developer to transfer the house on a 99-year lease for conversion into residential units. This proposed course of action was strongly opposed locally by those who felt that this important part of Hackney's history should be made properly accessible to the whole community.

The 18th-century room (now the shop) during refurbishment in 1991, drawn by Martin Shortis

The new conservatory in 1992, architect Richard Griffiths

The future

Lucy Medhurst, paint conservator, 1992

Following a successful campaign by local residents to persuade the National Trust to reverse its decision, a pressure group, the Sutton House Society, was founded in 1987. Over the next two years the Society and the Trust worked in partnership to devise a scheme whereby the house could be repaired and refurbished for community use. In December 1989 a local committee was formally constituted to implement the Sutton House Community Scheme. The three-year programme of work began in January 1990.

Ironically, during the time the house was in its most forlorn state – stripped of its panelling, bereft of some of its 18th-century grates and fire surrounds and decorated with squatters' graffiti – it began to reveal its true value.

Research into archives and libraries uncovered much of the history of the early occupants as recorded in this guide. A full structural survey undertaken by English Heritage (London Division) and archaeological research below ground by the Museum of London Archaeology Service have greatly expanded our knowledge of the structure of the house. All this research is being brought together in a comprehensive monograph to be published jointly by the National Trust and English Heritage.

The future of Sutton House is now assured. It is a focal point for discovering the heritage of Hackney and attracts visitors from all parts of the country, as well as from abroad. It is a valuable educational resource for local schools, enabling children to study life in a Tudor home. However, just as importantly, it is a lively cultural and social centre for the community. The Edwardian Wenlock Barn is regularly used for recitals and conferences and the historic rooms are in demand for small meetings and training sessions. Private use of the house can be enjoyed for weddings and other celebrations. The new café-bar is used by visitors and locals alike, and the shop has a good stock of local history publications and local craftware. This current phase takes its place within the long history of the house, from the late Middle Ages far into the next millennium. Just like its builder, Sir Ralph Sadleir, the house has proved to be a great survivor!

Loe & Company's team of craftsmen, with Richard Griffiths architect (top right), and Carole Mills, project manager, on completion of the first phase of restoration in August 1992